Incredibly Easy
Salads

Publications International, Ltd.
Favorite Brand Name Recipes at www.fbnr.com

Microwave Cooking: Microwave ovens vary in wattage. Use the cooking times as guidelines and check for doneness before adding more time.

Preparation/Cooking Times: Preparation times are based on the approximate amount of time required to assemble the recipe before cooking, baking, chilling or serving. These times include preparation steps such as measuring, chopping and mixing. The fact that some preparations and cooking can be done simultaneously is taken into account. Preparation of optional ingredients and serving suggestions is not included.

Contents

**Tomato and Sugar Snap
Salad (p. 28)**

**Roasted Shanghai
Pepper Salad (p. 18)**

Crunch a Bunch Salad
(p. 24)

Roasted Vegetable Salad
(p. 14)

Green and Leafy

Zucchini Salad

1 pound zucchini, unpeeled
1 medium sweet onion, sliced thinly
1 medium orange bell pepper, sliced
½ cup cider vinegar
⅓ cup water
1 tablespoon vegetable oil
½ cup EQUAL® SPOONFUL*
¼ teaspoon salt
¼ teaspoon ground black pepper
¼ teaspoon dried marjoram or tarragon, crushed (optional)
6 cups salad greens
12 arugula leaves
3 tablespoons pine nuts, optional

May substitute 12 packets EQUAL® sweetener.

• Cut zucchini into ⅛-inch slices. Combine with onion and bell pepper; set aside.

• Combine vinegar, water, oil, Equal®, salt, pepper and marjoram in quart-size container with lid. Pour over vegetables. Chill overnight.

• Spoon vegetables over salad greens using slotted spoon. Top with bits of arugula and sprinkle with pine nuts.   *Makes 6 servings*

Antipasti Focaccia Salad

Dressing
   ½ cup extra-virgin olive oil
   3 tablespoons red wine vinegar
   1 medium clove garlic, minced
   2 teaspoons dried basil
1½ teaspoons dried oregano
   ½ teaspoon salt
   ⅛ teaspoon red pepper flakes

Salad
   1 (9-ounce) loaf focaccia
   2 medium tomatoes, each cut into 4 slices
   1 can (7 ounces) hearts of palm, cut into ½-inch rounds
   1 bag (5 ounces) romaine or European blend lettuce
   8 slices hard salami, cut into thin strips
   2 ounces fresh mozzarella, cut into ½-inch cubes
   8 jumbo stuffed Spanish green olives

1. Combine dressing ingredients in medium jar with tight-fitting lid. Cover and shake until well blended; set aside.

2. Cut focaccia in half crosswise. Reserve one half for another use. Cut remaining half into 4 wedges. Place wedges on dinner plates. Spoon 1 tablespoon dressing evenly over wedges and let soak into bread. Top each wedge with 2 tomato slices.

3. Combine remaining salad ingredients in large bowl. Add remaining dressing; toss well. Mound equal amounts over each wedge of bread.

Makes 4 servings

Variations: Warm bread in microwave for a few seconds just before serving. Add 1 (15-ounce) can garbanzo beans, rinsed and drained, to salad.

Southwest Veggie Salad

Prep Time: 15 minutes • **Cook Time:** 17 to 19 minutes

4 frozen spicy black bean vegetarian burgers
¾ cup frozen corn
8 cups torn mixed salad greens
¾ cup chopped tomato
¼ cup sliced green onions
½ cup salsa
½ cup shredded Monterey Jack cheese or Mexican cheese blend
½ cup sour cream
1½ cups tortilla chips

1. Preheat oven to 375°F. Place frozen burgers on foil-lined baking sheet. Bake 17 to 19 minutes, turning halfway through cooking time.

2. Meanwhile, place corn in small microwavable bowl and loosely cover. Cook on HIGH 1 minute or until heated through. Drain off any liquid.

3. Combine greens, tomato and green onions in large bowl. Arrange on 4 serving plates; set aside.

4. Cut each burger into thin strips. Top each salad with burger strips and corn. Drizzle with salsa. Sprinkle with cheese. Top with sour cream. Serve with chips. *Makes 4 servings*

Crunchy Mexican Side Salad

3 cups romaine and iceberg lettuce blend
½ cup grape tomatoes, halved
½ cup peeled and diced jicama
¼ cup sliced ripe olives
¼ cup ORTEGA® Sliced Jalapeños, quartered
2 tablespoons ORTEGA® Taco Sauce
1 tablespoon vegetable oil
⅛ teaspoon salt
Crushed ORTEGA® Taco Shells (optional)

Toss together lettuce, tomatoes, jicama, olives and jalapeños in large bowl.

Combine taco sauce, oil and salt in small bowl. Stir with a fork until blended.

Pour dressing over salad; toss gently to coat. Top with taco shells, if desired.   *Makes 4 servings (1 cup each)*

Note: ORTEGA® Sliced Jalapeños are available in a 12-ounce jar. They are pickled, adding great flavor and crunch to this salad.

*Tip

There are many choices available when buying grape tomatoes these days. Look for yellow, orange and red varieties. All are equally sweet and perfectly sized for healthy snacking.

Roasted Vegetable Salad

1 cup sliced mushrooms
1 cup sliced carrots
1 cup chopped green or yellow bell pepper
1 cup cherry tomatoes, halved
½ cup chopped onion
2 tablespoons chopped pitted kalamata olives
2 teaspoons lemon juice, divided
1 teaspoon dried oregano
1 teaspoon olive oil
½ teaspoon black pepper
1 teaspoon salt
3 cups packed torn stemmed spinach or baby spinach

1. Preheat oven to 375°F. Combine mushrooms, carrots, bell pepper, tomatoes, onion, olives, 1 teaspoon lemon juice, oregano, oil and black pepper in large bowl; toss until evenly coated. Spread vegetables in single layer on baking sheet.

2. Bake 20 minutes, stirring once. Remove from oven; stir in remaining 1 teaspoon lemon juice and salt. Serve warm over spinach.

Makes 2 servings

Marinated
Antipasto

¼ **cup extra-virgin olive oil**
2 **tablespoons balsamic vinegar**
1 **clove garlic, minced**
½ **teaspoon sugar**
½ **teaspoon salt**
¼ **teaspoon black pepper**
1 **pint (2 cups) cherry tomatoes**
1 **can (14 ounces) quartered artichoke hearts, drained**
8 **ounces small balls or cubes fresh mozzarella cheese**
1 **cup drained pitted kalamata olives**
¼ **cup sliced fresh basil**
   Lettuce leaves

1. Whisk together oil, vinegar, garlic, sugar, salt and pepper in medium bowl. Add tomatoes, artichokes, mozzarella, olives and basil; toss to coat. Let stand at least 30 minutes.

2. Line platter with lettuce. Arrange tomato mixture over lettuce; serve at room temperature. *Makes about 5 cups*

Serving Suggestion: Serve antipasto with toothpicks as an appetizer or spoon over Bibb lettuce leaves for a first-course salad.

Roasted Shanghai Pepper Salad

1 jar (14 to 15 ounces) roasted red or yellow peppers
1½ tablespoons soy sauce
1 tablespoon rice vinegar
1 tablespoon dark sesame oil
2 teaspoons honey
1 clove garlic, minced
   Romaine lettuce or spinach leaves
2 tablespoons coarsely chopped fresh cilantro

1. Drain and rinse peppers; pat dry with paper towels. Cut peppers lengthwise into ½-inch strips; place in small bowl.

2. Combine soy sauce, vinegar, sesame oil, honey and garlic; mix well. Pour over peppers; cover and refrigerate at least 2 hours.

3. Serve over lettuce leaves. Sprinkle with cilantro.   *Makes 4 servings*

Note: This salad will keep up to 1 week covered and refrigerated.

Berry Spinach Salad

Prep Time: 15 minutes

6 cups fresh baby spinach
2 cups sliced fresh strawberries
2 tablespoons chopped red onion
⅓ cup raspberry vinaigrette
¼ teaspoon black pepper
¼ cup crumbled feta cheese

1. Combine spinach, strawberries and red onion in large bowl.

2. Whisk together vinaigrette and black pepper in small bowl. Drizzle over salad; toss to coat. Arrange evenly on 4 serving plates. Sprinkle evenly with cheese.

Makes 4 servings

Oriental Salad Supreme

¼ cup peanut or vegetable oil
¼ cup rice vinegar
2 tablespoons packed brown sugar
½ medium unpeeled cucumber, halved and sliced
6 cups torn romaine or leaf lettuce
1 cup chow mein noodles
¼ cup peanuts or coarsely chopped cashews (optional)

1. Combine oil, vinegar and brown sugar in small bowl; whisk until sugar dissolves.* Toss with cucumbers. Marinate, covered, in refrigerator up to 4 hours.

2. Just before serving, combine lettuce, chow mein noodles and peanuts, if desired, in large bowl. Add dressing; toss to combine.

Makes 4 servings

At this point, dressing may be tossed with remaining ingredients and served immediately.

Warm Mushroom Salad

12 ounces mixed salad greens (such as spinach, arugula, curly endive and romaine)

3 tablespoons FILIPPO BERIO® Olive Oil

1 (10-ounce) package mushrooms, cleaned and quartered or sliced

3 shallots, chopped

1 clove garlic, crushed

2 tablespoons chopped fresh chives

2 tablespoons lemon juice

2 tablespoons balsamic vinegar

1 teaspoon sugar

1½ cups purchased garlic croutons

Shavings of Parmesan cheese

Salt and freshly ground black pepper

Tear salad greens into bite-size pieces. Arrange on 4 serving plates. In medium skillet, heat olive oil over medium heat until hot. Add mushrooms, shallots and garlic; cook and stir 3 to 5 minutes or until mushrooms are soft. Stir in chives, lemon juice, vinegar and sugar; simmer 30 seconds. Spoon mixture over salad greens. Top with croutons and Parmesan cheese. Season to taste with salt and pepper.

Makes 4 to 6 servings

Greens and Pear with Maple-Mustard Dressing

Prep Time: 15 minutes

¼ cup maple syrup
1 tablespoon Dijon mustard
1 tablespoon olive oil
1 tablespoon balsamic or cider vinegar
⅛ teaspoon black pepper
4 cups torn mixed salad greens
1 medium red pear, cored and thinly sliced
¼ cup sliced green onions
3 tablespoons dried cherries
8 teaspoons chopped walnuts, toasted*

To toast walnuts, spread in single layer on baking sheet. Bake in preheated 350°F oven 5 to 7 minutes or until fragrant, stirring occasionally.

1. Whisk together syrup, mustard, oil, vinegar and pepper in small bowl.

2. Combine greens, pear slices, green onions, cherries and walnuts in large salad bowl. Drizzle with syrup mixture; toss gently.

Makes 4 servings

*Tip

Chose a pear that is slightly underripe for this salad. That way it will hold its shape and not break into pieces.

Garden Fresh Salad

5 cups assorted lettuce leaves
½ cup bell pepper slices
½ cup cherry or grape tomatoes
½ small cucumber, sliced
½ red onion, sliced
¼ cup sliced radishes
   Fresh thyme or parsley
   Creamy Garlic Dressing (page 148)

Divide salad ingredients evenly among individual bowls. Top with dressing.

Makes 4 servings

Crunch a Bunch Salad

2 tablespoons honey or sugar
1 tablespoon apple cider vinegar
1 tablespoon vegetable oil
½ teaspoon soy sauce or lemon juice
1 cup sugar snap peas, trimmed
1 carrot, peeled and thinly sliced
1 stalk celery, sliced
3 radishes, thinly sliced
4 cherry tomatoes, cut into quarters
4 teaspoons sliced almonds

1. Whisk honey, vinegar, oil and soy sauce in small bowl until well blended.

2. Divide vegetables among 4 individual serving dishes. Top with almonds. Drizzle with dressing or serve on the side for dipping.

Makes 4 servings

Grilled Beet Salad

6 medium red beets (about 1½ pounds), peeled
1 medium yellow onion, cut into ½-inch wedges
½ pound carrots, halved lengthwise and cut into 1-inch pieces
¼ cup plus 2 tablespoons olive oil, divided
3 to 4 tablespoons balsamic vinegar
½ teaspoon dried rosemary
1 clove garlic, minced
½ teaspoon salt
¼ teaspoon black pepper
6 cups chopped spring greens *or* 2 packages (5 ounces each)
1 cup pecan pieces, toasted* or candied pecans
½ cup (2 ounces) Gorgonzola or goat cheese, crumbled

*To toast pecans, spread in single layer on baking sheet and toast in preheated 350°F oven for 8 to 10 minutes or until very lightly browned.

1. Prepare grill for direct cooking over medium-high heat.

2. Cut beets into 1-inch pieces; place in microwaveable dish. Cover; microwave on HIGH 6 to 8 minutes or until slightly soft. Uncover; cool to room temperature. Pat beets dry with paper towels.

3. Divide beets, onions and carrots evenly between two 12×8 disposable foil pans. Arrange vegetables in single layer. Drizzle each pan with 1 tablespoon oil; toss to coat vegetables. Cover loosely with foil. Place pans on grid over medium-high heat. Grill 22 to 25 minutes, stirring every few minutes until fork-tender. Cool completely.

4. To make vinaigrette, combine remaining ¼ cup oil, vinegar, rosemary, garlic, salt and pepper in small bowl; mix well.

5. Arrange greens in salad bowl or on platter. Add half of vinaigrette; toss gently. Top with grilled vegetables; drizzle with remaining vinaigrette. Garnish with pecans and cheese. Serve immediately.   *Makes 4 servings*

Note: To peel beets, trim ends, then peel with a vegetable peeler under running water to help minimize beet juice from staining hands.

Tomato and Sugar Snap Salad

8 ounces fresh sugar snap peas, or green beans, trimmed
2 medium tomatoes, cut into ½-inch wedges
¼ cup thinly sliced red onions
¼ cup balsamic salad dressing
2 tablespoons chopped fresh basil or parsley
¼ teaspoon salt
½ cup (2 ounces) crumbled feta cheese

1. Cook snap peas in vegetable steamer 3 minutes or until crisp-tender. Rinse with cold water until cool. Drain well.

2. Combine peas, tomatoes, onions, salad dressing, basil and salt in medium bowl. Toss gently until coated. Sprinkle with feta.

Makes 8 servings

Mixed Greens with Pecans, Cranberries & Goat Cheese

⅓ cup extra-virgin olive oil
2 tablespoons balsamic or cider vinegar
1 tablespoon sugar
¼ teaspoon salt
⅛ teaspoon red pepper flakes
1 package (5 ounces) mixed greens
½ cup pecan halves, toasted
⅓ cup thinly sliced red onion
⅓ cup dried cranberries or cherries
½ cup (2 ounces) crumbled goat cheese

1. Combine oil, vinegar, sugar, salt and red pepper flakes in small jar with tight-fitting lid. Shake vigorously until well blended.

2. Combine greens, pecans, onion, cranberries and dressing in serving bowl; toss gently. Sprinkle with cheese. *Makes 6 to 8 servings*

**Gazpacho Steak Salad
(p. 42)**

**Jerked Pork &
Mango Salad (p. 36)**

Pastrami and Radish
Salad (p. 44)

Chinese Chicken Salad
(p. 34)

Main Dish **Meat**

Sirloin Steak Antipasto Salad

3 cloves garlic, minced
½ teaspoon black pepper
1 boneless beef top sirloin steak (about 1 pound and ¾-inch thick), trimmed of fat
8 cups torn romaine lettuce
16 cherry tomatoes, halved
16 pitted kalamata olives, halved lengthwise
1 can (14 ounces) quartered artichoke hearts in water, rinsed and drained
⅓ cup Greek Vinaigrette (page 151)
¼ cup fresh basil, cut into thin strips

1. Prepare grill for direct cooking or preheat broiler.

2. Sprinkle garlic and pepper over steak. Grill over medium-hot coals or broil 4 inches from heat 4 minutes per side for medium-rare or until desired doneness. Transfer steak to carving board. Tent with foil. Let stand at least 5 minutes.

3. Meanwhile, combine romaine, tomatoes, olives and artichoke hearts in large bowl. Add dressing; toss well. Transfer to 4 plates. Carve steak crosswise into thin slices; arrange over salads. Drizzle juices from carving board over steak. Sprinkle with basil. *Makes 4 servings*

Chinese Chicken Salad

4 cups chopped bok choy
3 cups diced cooked chicken breast
1 cup shredded carrots
2 tablespoons minced fresh chives or green onions
2 tablespoons hot chile sauce with garlic*
1½ tablespoons peanut or canola oil
1 tablespoon balsamic vinegar
1 tablespoon soy sauce
1 teaspoon minced fresh ginger

Hot chile sauce with garlic is available in the Asian foods section of most supermarkets.

1. Place bok choy, chicken, carrots and chives in large bowl.

2. Combine chile garlic sauce, oil, vinegar, soy sauce and ginger in small bowl; mix well. Pour over chicken mixture; toss gently.

Makes 4 servings

*Tip

Bok choy is a mild Chinese vegetable with crunchy white stems and dark green leaves. Slice it and add to salads or throw some into the wok for a great addition to a stir-fry.

Jerked Pork & Mango Salad

2½ teaspoons Caribbean jerk seasoning, divided
1 boneless pork tenderloin (1 pound), trimmed of fat
   Nonstick cooking spray
8 cups mesclun or spring salad greens
1 ripe mango, diced
½ cup sliced green onions
**2 tablespoons plus 2 teaspoons mango chutney, large pieces
   of mango chopped**
2 tablespoons canola or peanut oil
1 tablespoon plus 1½ teaspoons fresh lime juice
¼ teaspoon salt
½ cup chopped fresh cilantro

1. Prepare grill for direct cooking or preheat broiler.

2. Sprinkle 2 teaspoons seasoning over all sides of pork; coat with cooking spray. Grill pork over medium heat or broil 4 inches from heat source 6 to 7 minutes per side or until pork is barely pink in center (155°F). Transfer pork to carving board. Tent with foil and let stand at least 5 minutes. Internal temperature will continue to rise about 5°F.

3. Meanwhile, combine greens, mango and green onions in large bowl. Combine chutney, oil, lime juice, remaining ½ teaspoon seasoning and salt in small bowl; mix well. Add to greens mixture; toss well.

4. Transfer salad to dinner plates. Slice pork crosswise into thin slices; arrange over salads. Drizzle any juices from carving board over pork. Sprinkle with cilantro.   *Makes 4 servings*

Cobb
Salad

1 package (10 ounces) torn mixed salad greens *or*
    8 cups torn romaine
6 ounces cooked chicken breast, cut into bite-size pieces
1 tomato, seeded and chopped
2 hard-cooked eggs, cut into bite-size pieces
4 slices bacon, crisp-cooked and crumbled
1 ripe avocado, peeled and diced
1 large carrot, shredded
½ cup (2 ounces) blue cheese, crumbled
    Blue cheese dressing (optional)

1. Place lettuce in serving bowl. Arrange chicken, tomato, eggs, bacon, avocado, carrot and blue cheese on top of lettuce.

2. Serve with dressing, if desired.

Makes 4 servings

*Tip

The Cobb Salad was made famous by Hollywood's Brown Derby Restaurant. The main ingredients of chicken, bacon, eggs, avocado and blue cheese are fairly standard.

Santa Fe BBQ Ranch Salad

Prep Time: 15 minutes • **Cook Time:** 10 minutes

1 cup Cattlemen's® Golden Honey Barbecue Sauce, divided
½ cup ranch salad dressing
1 pound boneless, skinless chicken
12 cups washed and torn Romaine lettuce
1 small red onion, thinly sliced
1 small ripe avocado, diced ½-inch
4 ripe plum tomatoes, sliced
2 cups shredded Monterey Jack cheese
½ cup cooked, crumbled bacon

1. Prepare BBQ Ranch Dressing: Combine ½ cup barbecue sauce and salad dressing in small bowl; reserve.

2. Grill or broil chicken over medium-high heat 10 minutes until no longer pink in center. Cut into strips and toss with remaining ½ cup barbecue sauce.

3. Toss lettuce, onion, avocado, tomatoes, cheese and bacon in large bowl. Portion on salad plates, dividing evenly. Top with chicken and serve with BBQ Ranch Dressing. *Makes 4 servings*

Tip: Serve **Cattlemen's®** Golden Honey Barbecue Sauce as a dipping sauce with chicken nuggets or seafood kabobs.

Gazpacho Steak Salad

Prep and Cook Time: 30 minutes • **Marinate Time:** 6 hours or overnight

- **1 pound beef shoulder steak or 1 pound beef top round steak, cut 1 inch thick**
- **1 can (5½ ounces) spicy 100% vegetable juice**
- **8 cups mixed greens *or* 1 package (10 ounces) romaine and leaf lettuce mixture**
- **1 cup baby pear tomatoes, halved**
- **1 cup cucumber, cut in half lengthwise, then into thin slices**
- **1 cup chopped green bell pepper**
- **Salt and pepper**
- **Crunchy Tortilla Strips (recipe follows)**

Gazpacho Dressing
- **1 can (5½ ounces) spicy 100% vegetable juice**
- **½ cup chopped tomato**
- **¼ cup finely chopped green bell pepper**
- **1 tablespoon red wine vinegar**
- **1 tablespoon chopped cilantro**
- **2 teaspoons olive oil**
- **1 clove garlic, minced**

1. Place beef steak and 1 can vegetable juice in food-safe plastic bag; turn steak to coat. Close bag securely and marinate in refrigerator 6 hours or as long as overnight.

2. Combine dressing ingredients; refrigerate. Combine greens, baby pear tomatoes, cucumber and 1 cup green bell pepper; refrigerate.

3. Remove steak from marinade; discard marinade. Place steak on grid over medium, ash-covered coals. Grill shoulder steaks, uncovered, 16 to 20 minutes for medium rare to medium doneness (top round steak 16 to 18 minutes for medium rare doneness; do not overcook), turning occasionally. Carve steak across the grain into thin slices. Season with salt and pepper, as desired.

4. Meanwhile prepare Crunchy Tortilla Strips. Add steak to salad mixture. Drizzle with dressing and top with tortilla strips.   *Makes 4 servings*

Crunchy Tortilla Strips: Heat oven to 400°F. Cut 2 corn tortillas in half, then crosswise into ¼-inch wide strips. Place strips in single layer on baking sheet. Bake 4 to 8 minutes or until crisp.

Favorite recipe from **The Beef Checkoff**

Beef Caesar Salad

1 bag (10 ounces) chopped romaine lettuce
2 tablespoons Caesar Dressing (page 152)
1 pound boneless beef top sirloin steak
   Nonstick cooking spray
   Black pepper
2 slices whole wheat bread, toasted and cut into 32 squares

1. Toss romaine and dressing in large bowl. Divide salad greens evenly among 4 plates.

2. Cut steak lengthwise in half, then crosswise into ⅛-inch-thick strips. Spray large nonstick skillet with cooking spray and heat over high heat. Add beef; cook and stir 2 minutes or until beef is tender.

3. Top salads with steak strips. Season with pepper and top with croutons.
                                      Makes 4 servings

Pastrami and Radish Salad

    1 bunch radishes
    ½ pound JENNIE-O TURKEY STORE® Turkey Pastrami, cut into
       strips
    1 shallot, finely chopped
    1 head leaf lettuce, torn into bite-size pieces
    1 can (14 ounces) artichoke hearts, drained and cut into
       halves
    6 tablespoons red wine vinegar
    1 clove garlic, minced
 1½ tablespoons poppy seeds
    Salt and pepper to taste

Trim radishes and make several cuts in each one for an accordion effect. Place radishes in bowl of ice water to help them open up. In large serving bowl, combine turkey pastrami, shallot, lettuce and artichoke hearts. Measure oil, vinegar, garlic, poppy seeds, salt and pepper into small jar with tight-fitting lid; shake until well blended. Pour dressing over salad; toss well. Drain radishes, add to salad.   *Makes 3 to 4 main-dish servings*

Citrus Pork Tenderloin & Spinach Salad

Prep Time: 15 minutes • **Cook Time:** 30 minutes

1 pound pork tenderloin
½ cup orange juice
¼ cup *French's*® Honey Mustard
12 cups baby spinach leaves and/or mixed field greens
1½ cups orange segments (about 3 medium oranges)
1⅓ cups *French's*® French Fried Onions
½ red bell pepper, cut into strips

1. Preheat oven to 425°F. Season pork with salt and pepper. Roast* pork for 30 minutes or until meat reaches internal temperature of 160°F. Cool slightly. Cut into ¼-inch-thick slices.

2. Combine orange juice and mustard in small bowl; set aside. Arrange salad greens evenly on serving plates. Top with pork, oranges and French Fried Onions, dividing evenly. Garnish salad with bell pepper and serve with mustard dressing. Serve immediately.

*Or grill meat over medium heat for 30 minutes, turning often.

Makes 6 servings

*Tip

For extra crispiness, heat ***French's*®** French Fried Onions in microwave for 1 minute.

Ginger-Teriyaki Salad with Fried Chicken Tenders

12 ounces frozen breaded chicken tenders
1 bag (5 ounces) spring greens mix
1 cup (2 ounces) broccoli florets
1 cup (3 ounces) carrots, cut into matchstick-size strips
½ cup chopped green onions
½ cup Sesame Vinaigrette (page 150)
¼ cup peanuts, toasted

1. Bake chicken tenders according to package directions. Cool 5 minutes. Cut into ½-inch pieces.

2. Combine spring greens mix, broccoli, carrots and green onions in large bowl. Add salad dressing; toss to coat.

3. Spoon onto 4 plates and top with equal amounts chicken pieces and peanuts. *Makes 4 servings*

*Tip

To toast peanuts, heat a small skillet over medium-high heat. Add peanuts and cook and stir 3 minutes or until fragrant and beginning to brown. Immediately remove from skillet.

Healthy Chopped Salad

10 ounces cooked skinless turkey breast
1 small head bok choy, chopped
2 cups baby spinach, chopped
1 tomato, chopped
1 cup baby carrots, chopped
1 package (8 ounces) sugar snap peas, chopped
2 romaine lettuce hearts, chopped
  Juice of 1 lemon (about ¼ cup)
  Juice of 1 lime (about ¼ cup)
1 tablespoon creamy peanut butter
2 teaspoons sugar
2 teaspoons sesame seeds
1 teaspoon chopped garlic
½ teaspoon black pepper

1. Place turkey, bok choy, spinach, tomato, carrots, snap peas and romaine in large bowl; set aside.

2. Combine lemon juice, lime juice, peanut butter, sugar, sesame seeds, garlic and black pepper in small jar with tight-fitting lid; shake until well blended.

3. Pour dressing over salad; toss well. *Makes 8 servings*

Serving Suggestion: For company, instead of tossing the salad in a bowl, lay lines of chopped ingredients across a large serving platter. Toss the salad at the table on the platter, or leave it untossed and let guests select their ingredients. Pass the dressing at the table.

Jerk Turkey
Salad

6 ounces boneless turkey breast tenderloins or turkey breast cutlets
1½ teaspoons Caribbean jerk seasoning
4 cups mixed salad greens
¾ cup sliced peeled cucumber
⅔ cup chopped fresh pineapple
⅔ cup raspberries or quartered strawberries
½ cup slivered peeled jicama or sliced celery
1 green onion, sliced
¼ cup lime juice
3 tablespoons honey

1. Prepare grill for direct cooking. Rub turkey with jerk seasoning.

2. Grill turkey over medium coals 15 to 20 minutes or until turkey is cooked through, turning once. Remove from grill and cool.

3. Cut turkey into bite-size pieces. Toss together turkey, greens, cucumber, pineapple, raspberries, jicama and green onion.

4. Combine lime juice and honey. Toss with greens mixture. Serve immediately. *Makes 2 servings*

Tropical Curried Chicken Salad

Prep Time: 15 minutes • **Cook Time:** 15 minutes
Marinate Time: 30 minutes

⅔ **cup prepared olive oil vinaigrette salad dressing**
¼ **cup** *French's*® **Worcestershire Sauce**
¼ **cup honey**
2 **tablespoons** *Frank's*® *RedHot*® **Cayenne Pepper Sauce**
2 **teaspoons curry powder**
2 **cloves garlic, minced**
1 **pound boneless, skinless chicken breasts**
8 **cups washed and torn watercress and Boston lettuce**
¼ **cup coarsely chopped unsalted cashew nuts**
½ **cup shredded coconut, toasted**

1. Place salad dressing, Worcestershire, honey, *Frank's*® *RedHot*® Sauce, curry and garlic in blender or food processor. Cover; process until well blended. Reserve ½ cup curry mixture to dress salad.

2. Place chicken in large resealable plastic food storage bag. Pour remaining curry mixture over chicken. Seal bag; marinate in refrigerator 30 minutes.

3. Heat electric grill pan or barbecue grill. Remove chicken from marinade; discard marinade. Grill chicken 10 to 15 minutes or until no longer pink in center (165°F). Arrange salad greens on large serving platter. Cut chicken into thin slices. Arrange over greens. Top with nuts and coconut. Serve with reserved dressing. *Makes 4 servings*

Shrimp Taco Salad with Chile Dressing (p. 56)

Warm Blackened Tuna Salad (p. 74)

Grilled Salmon Salad
(p. 58)

Fish Taco Salad
(p. 76)

Simply Seafood

Shrimp Taco Salad with Chile Dressing

Prep Time: 5 minutes • **Start to Finish:** 20 minutes

2 tablespoons butter
1 pound raw shrimp (21 to 30 count), peeled, deveined
1 cup ORTEGA® Taco Sauce
½ cup sour cream
¼ cup milk
3 tablespoons ORTEGA® Diced Green Chiles
   Salt and black pepper, to taste
1 head iceberg lettuce, chopped
6 ORTEGA® Yellow Corn Taco Shells, crumbled
½ cup shredded Cheddar cheese

Melt butter in skillet over medium heat. Add shrimp and taco sauce; cook until shrimp are cooked through and pink, about 5 minutes.

For Chile Dressing, combine sour cream, milk, chiles, salt and pepper. Toss lettuce with dressing and top with crumbled taco shells, shrimp and shredded cheese.   *Makes 6 servings*

Serving Suggestion: Try serving Shrimp Taco Salad in your favorite Ortega® soft or hard taco.

Grilled Salmon Salad

⅓ cup plus 2 tablespoons Raspberry Vinaigrette (page 148), divided
4 skinless salmon fillets (4 ounces each)
½ teaspoon black pepper
¼ teaspoon salt
8 cups spring salad greens
2 cups cherry tomatoes, halved
¼ cup fresh basil, chopped (optional)

1. Prepare grill for direct cooking. Brush 2 tablespoons dressing over salmon. Sprinkle with pepper and salt. Grill salmon on covered grill over medium-high heat 5 to 6 minutes or until center is opaque.

2. Combine greens, tomatoes and remaining ⅓ cup dressing in large bowl; toss gently. Transfer to 4 plates. Top with salmon; sprinkle with basil, if desired. *Makes 4 servings*

Note: To broil the salmon, preheat the broiler. Place salmon on an oiled broiler pan. Broil 4 inches from heat 6 to 7 minutes or just until the salmon begins to flake when tested with a fork.

Warm Shrimp, Artichoke & Parmesan Salad

1 can (14 ounces) water-packed quartered artichoke hearts
20 frozen cooked tail-on premium shrimp (12 ounces)
½ cup Italian salad dressing
1 bag (12 ounces) salad blend
¼ cup (1 ounce) grated Parmesan cheese

1. Drain and rinse artichoke hearts. Combine with shrimp and dressing in large, deep skillet. Cover and cook over medium heat 10 minutes, stirring occasionally.

2. Divide salad blend between 4 dinner plates. Top salad with shrimp-artichoke mixture. Sprinkle with cheese. *Makes 4 servings*

Calamari Salad

¼ cup plus 1 tablespoon extra-virgin olive oil, divided
1½ pounds cleaned fresh squid, bodies only
   Juice of 1 lemon
1 can (about 15 ounces) cannellini beans, rinsed and drained
1 cup thinly sliced celery
1 cup thinly sliced red bell pepper
½ cup thinly sliced white onion
3 tablespoons red wine vinegar
2 tablespoons chopped fresh Italian parsley
1 tablespoon chopped fresh basil
1 tablespoon chopped fresh oregano
2 cloves garlic, finely chopped
1 teaspoon salt
½ teaspoon red pepper flakes

1. Heat 1 tablespoon oil in large nonstick skillet over medium-high heat. Cook squid about 2 minutes per side. Let cool slightly; cut into rings. Place in large bowl; drizzle with lemon juice. Add beans, celery, bell pepper and onion.

2. Whisk together vinegar, parsley, basil, oregano, garlic, salt and red pepper flakes in small bowl. Slowly whisk in remaining ¼ cup oil until blended. Pour dressing over squid mixture and toss gently. Refrigerate at least 1 hour. Serve chilled or at room temperature. *Makes 6 servings*

Grilled Lobster, Shrimp and Calamari Seviche

¾ cup orange juice
⅓ cup fresh lime juice
2 jalapeño peppers,* seeded and minced
2 tablespoons chopped fresh cilantro, chives or green onion
2 tablespoons tequila
1 teaspoon honey
1 teaspoon ground cumin
1 teaspoon olive oil
10 squid, cleaned and cut into rings and tentacles
½ pound medium raw shrimp, peeled and deveined
2 lobster tails (8 ounces each), meat removed and shells discarded

*Jalapeño peppers can sting and irritate the skin, so wear rubber gloves when handling peppers and do not touch your eyes.

1. For marinade, combine orange juice, lime juice, jalapeños, cilantro, tequila and honey in medium glass bowl.

2. Measure ¼ cup marinade into small bowl; stir in cumin and oil. Reserve. Refrigerate remaining marinade.

3. Prepare grill for direct cooking.

4. Bring 1 quart water to a boil in large saucepan over high heat. Add squid; cook 30 seconds or until opaque. Drain. Rinse under cold water; drain. Add squid to refrigerated marinade.

5. Thread shrimp onto metal skewers. Brush shrimp and lobster with reserved ¼ cup marinade.

6. Place shrimp on grid. Grill shrimp, uncovered, over medium-high heat 2 to 3 minutes per side or until pink and opaque. Remove shrimp from skewers; add to squid. Place lobster on grid. Grill 5 minutes per side or until meat turns opaque and is cooked through. Slice lobster meat into ¼-inch-thick slices; add to squid and shrimp mixture.

7. Refrigerate at least 2 hours or overnight.

Makes 8 appetizer servings

Easy Tossed Niçoise with Garlic and Cheese Dressing

1½ pounds steamed red potatoes, cut into small chunks
1 package (10 ounces) frozen Italian green beans, thawed and drained
¾ cup niçoise or pitted ripe olives, sliced
½ red onion, slivered
½ red bell pepper, slivered
½ green bell pepper, slivered
¼ cup coarsely chopped green onions, including tops
1½ cups Garlic and Cheese Dressing (recipe follows)
1 (7-ounce) STARKIST Flavor Fresh Pouch® Tuna (Albacore)
½ cup minced fresh parsley
Whole romaine leaves, washed and dried
Freshly ground black pepper (optional)
Grated Parmesan cheese (optional)

In large bowl, combine potatoes, beans, olives, red onion, bell peppers and green onions; toss with Garlic and Cheese Dressing. Refrigerate. Just before serving, add tuna and parsley. Line plates with lettuce; spoon salad onto leaves. Serve with black pepper and cheese, if desired.

Makes 6 to 8 servings

Garlic and Cheese Dressing

¼ cup wine vinegar
2 tablespoons lemon juice
1 to 2 cloves garlic, minced or pressed
1 tablespoon Dijon-style mustard
Salt and black pepper to taste
1 cup olive oil
½ cup grated Parmesan cheese

In small bowl, whisk together vinegar, lemon juice, garlic, mustard, salt and pepper. Slowly add olive oil, whisking until all oil is added and dressing is thickened. Stir in cheese.

Salmon, Asparagus & Orzo Salad

1 (8-ounce) salmon fillet
1 cup uncooked orzo pasta
8 ounces asparagus spears, cut into 2-inch lengths (about 1½ cups), cooked
½ cup dried cranberries
¼ cup sliced green onions
3 tablespoons extra-virgin olive oil
1 tablespoon white wine vinegar
1½ teaspoons Dijon mustard
½ teaspoon salt
⅛ teaspoon black pepper

1. Prepare grill for direct cooking. Grill salmon on oiled grid over medium coals about 10 minutes per inch of thickness or until opaque. Remove from grill; cool. Flake salmon into bite-size pieces.

2. Meanwhile, cook orzo according to package directions; drain and cool.

3. Combine salmon, orzo, asparagus, cranberries and green onions in large bowl. Whisk together olive oil, vinegar, mustard, salt and pepper in small bowl until well blended. Pour over salmon mixture; toss until coated. Chill 30 minutes to 1 hour. *Makes 4 servings*

*Tip

Asparagus season ranges from February to June. Look for asparagus with firm purplish-green heads. Keep asparagus wrapped in damp paper towels in your refrigerator for up to 2 days.

Warm Thai-Style Scallop & Mango Salad

Prep Time: 20 minutes • **Cook Time:** 3 minutes

12 ounces bay scallops, rinsed and drained or medium shrimp, shelled and deveined

6 tablespoons oriental or oriental chicken salad dressing, divided

1 package (10 ounces) DOLE® Organic Salad Blend Baby Lettuces or Spring Mix with Herbs Salad

1 DOLE® Mango or Papaya, peeled, seeded, and chopped

1 medium cucumber, peeled, seeded and cut into half-slices

1 red, yellow or green bell pepper, cut into julienne strips

¼ cup cilantro leaves

• Cook scallops in 1 tablespoon salad dressing for 2 to 3 minutes just until opaque. (If using shrimp, cook until shrimp turn pink and opaque.) Remove from heat.

• Toss together salad blend, mango, cucumber, bell pepper and cilantro leaves with ¼ cup salad dressing. Spoon mixture onto three serving plates.

• Arrange scallops over each salad; drizzle remaining 1 tablespoon dressing over scallops.

Makes 3 servings

Grilled Tuna Salad with Avocado Dressing

Prep Time: 30 minutes • **Start to Finish:** 50 minutes

1 packet (1.25 ounces) ORTEGA® Taco Seasoning Mix
½ cup water
1½ pounds tuna steaks
1 ripe avocado
¼ cup ORTEGA® Salsa, any variety
¼ cup sour cream
Juice of ½ lime
½ teaspoon POLANER® Chopped Garlic
½ teaspoon salt
2 heads romaine lettuce, chopped
Salt and black pepper, to taste

Combine seasoning mix and water in shallow pan. Place tuna steaks in pan. Turn over to coat well. Marinate, covered, 15 minutes in refrigerator. Turn tuna steaks over again and marinate in refrigerator 15 minutes longer.

Preheat grill until piping hot, about 15 minutes. Grill tuna steaks 4 minutes on each side (fish will be pink on inside). Grill longer for well-done fish, if desired.

For Avocado Dressing, slice and pit avocado; scrape avocado flesh into small bowl. Add salsa, sour cream, lime juice, garlic and salt. Mix with fork, mashing avocado to combine ingredients well. Toss with chopped lettuce. Divide mixture among serving plates.

Slice tuna steaks into strips and place on lettuce. Add salt and pepper to taste.   *Makes 6 servings*

Note: Avocado Dressing can also be served with taco chips as Avocado-Salsa Dip. For taco chips, preheat oven to 350°F. Place ORTEGA® Yellow Corn Taco Shells on baking sheet and bake 10 minutes. Remove from oven and gently break into pieces. Sprinkle with salt, if desired. Serve with dip.

Mediterranean Shrimp and Feta Spring Salad

1 pound large raw shrimp, peeled and deveined with tails intact
1 teaspoon salt
4 cups (6 ounces) baby spinach
2 large plum tomatoes, cored and chopped
2 ounces feta cheese, crumbled
¼ cup chopped green onions
¼ cup coarsely chopped pitted kalamata olives
1 tablespoon minced fresh oregano or basil
3 tablespoons extra-virgin olive oil
1 tablespoon red wine vinegar
1 tablespoon small capers
½ teaspoon ground black pepper

1. Place shrimp in large saucepan with 1 quart of water. Add salt; bring to simmer over medium-high heat. Simmer 5 to 8 minutes or until shrimp are pink and opaque. Drain and set aside until cool enough to handle.

2. Place shrimp in large serving bowl. Add spinach, tomatoes, feta, green onions, olives and oregano. Combine olive oil, vinegar, capers and pepper in small bowl; mix well. Pour over salad; toss gently to coat.

Makes 4 servings

*Tip

Feta cheese can be made from cow's milk or goat's milk. Originally feta was made in Greece, but today you can find many wonderful domestic varieties.

Grilled Shrimp Salad
with Hot Bacon Vinaigrette

Prep Time: 10 minutes • **Cook Time:** 5 minutes

4 strips bacon, chopped
½ cup prepared Italian or vinaigrette salad dressing
⅓ cup *French's*® Honey Dijon Mustard or *French's*® Honey Mustard
2 tablespoons water
8 cups mixed salad greens
1 cup diced yellow bell peppers
1 cup halved cherry tomatoes
½ cup pine nuts
1 pound jumbo or extra large shrimp, shelled with tails on

1. Cook bacon until crisp in medium skillet. Whisk in salad dressing, mustard and water; keep warm over very low heat.

2. Place salad greens, bell peppers, tomatoes and pine nuts in large bowl; toss. Arrange on salad plates.

3. Cook shrimp in an electric grill pan or barbecue grill 3 minutes or until pink. Arrange on salads, dividing evenly. Serve with dressing.

Makes 4 servings

Warm Blackened Tuna Salad

    5 cups torn romaine lettuce
    2 cups coarsely shredded red cabbage
    2 medium yellow or green bell peppers, cut into strips
1½ cups sliced zucchini
    1 teaspoon onion powder
    ½ teaspoon garlic powder
    ½ teaspoon ground red pepper
    ½ teaspoon dried thyme
    ½ teaspoon black pepper
    ¾ pound fresh or thawed frozen tuna steaks, cut 1 inch thick
    ⅓ cup water
    ¾ cup sliced onion
    2 tablespoons balsamic vinegar
1½ teaspoons Dijon mustard
    1 teaspoon canola or vegetable oil
    ½ teaspoon chicken bouillon granules

1. Preheat broiler. Spray broiler pan with nonstick cooking spray. Combine romaine, cabbage, bell peppers and zucchini in large bowl; set aside.

2. Combine onion powder, garlic powder, red pepper, thyme and black pepper in small bowl. Rub spice mixture onto both sides of tuna. Place tuna on broiler pan. Broil 4 inches from heat about 10 minutes or until of desired degree of doneness, turning halfway through broiling time. Cover and set aside.

3. For dressing, bring water to a boil in small saucepan over high heat. Add onion slices; reduce heat to medium-low. Cover and simmer 4 to 5 minutes or until onion is tender. Add vinegar, mustard, oil and bouillon granules; cook and stir until heated through.

4. Place romaine mixture on 4 salad plates; slice tuna and arrange on top. Drizzle with dressing. Serve warm. *Makes 4 servings*

Fish Taco Salad

2 cups shredded romaine lettuce
1 medium cucumber, seeded and chopped
⅔ cup cherry or grape tomatoes, halved
½ cup chopped celery
¾ cup (about 6 ounces) flaked cooked cod or other firm white fish
Juice of ½ lime
1 tablespoon olive oil
¼ teaspoon black pepper
¼ cup sour cream
¼ cup salsa
1 teaspoon sugar
11 to 15 corn tortilla chips (about 1 ounce)

1. Layer romaine, cucumber, tomatoes, celery and fish in large bowl.

2. Whisk together lime juice, olive oil and pepper in small bowl. Pour dressing over salad; toss lightly. Divide salad evenly between 2 serving plates.

3. Whisk together sour cream, salsa and sugar in small bowl. Pour evenly down center of each salad. Crumble tortilla chips; sprinkle down each side of sour cream mixture.

Makes 2 servings

**BLT Salad with Bow Ties
& Cheddar (p. 90)**

**Traditional German
Potato Salad (p. 80)**

**Diner Egg Salad
Sandwich (p. 84)**

**Pounceole Salad
(p. 88)**

Picnic **Perfection**

Traditional German Potato Salad

2½ pounds red potatoes
¼ pound sliced bacon
½ medium onion, finely chopped
½ cup cider vinegar
¼ cup water
1 tablespoon plus 1 teaspoon sugar
1 teaspoon salt
1 teaspoon brown mustard seeds
1 teaspoon mustard
2 tablespoons finely chopped fresh parsley
1 teaspoon paprika

1. Place potatoes in large saucepan. Add enough water to cover. Bring to a boil over high heat. Reduce heat; simmer, uncovered, 20 to 30 minutes or until potatoes are fork-tender. Drain. Let potatoes cool.

2. Cook bacon in medium skillet over medium heat until crisp. Remove with slotted spoon. Crumble into small bowl; set aside. Drain all but 3 tablespoons drippings from skillet.

3. Cook and stir onion in same skillet. Peel potatoes and cut into ¼-inch slices.

4. Combine vinegar, water, sugar, salt, mustard seeds and mustard in large bowl. Add potatoes and bacon to vinegar mixture; toss to coat evenly. Top with parsley and sprinkle with paprika. Serve hot or cold.

Makes 6 to 8 servings

Note: This salad contains no eggs or mayonnaise and will keep well for picnics and other outdoor meals.

Spicy Citrus Slaw

Prep Time: 15 Minutes

1 cup HELLMANN'S® or BEST FOODS® Canola Cholesterol Free Mayonnaise
1 can (11 ounces) mandarin oranges, drained (reserve 2 tablespoons syrup)
2 teaspoons apple cider vinegar
1 tablespoon chopped fresh cilantro (optional)
   Hot pepper sauce to taste
½ teaspoon salt
1 bag (16 ounces) coleslaw mix

1. In large bowl, combine Hellmann's or Best Foods Canola Cholesterol Free Mayonnaise, reserved syrup, vinegar, cilantro, hot pepper sauce and salt. Stir in coleslaw mix and oranges. Chill, if desired.   *Makes 4 cups*

Four-Season Pasta Salad

8 ounces uncooked trumpet-shaped or spiral pasta
1½ cups cauliflower florets
1½ cups sliced carrots
1½ cups snow peas
½ cup Italian or honey-mustard salad dressing

1. Cook pasta according to package directions, adding cauliflower, carrots and snow peas to saucepan during last 3 minutes of cooking time. Drain pasta and vegetables. Place under cold running water to stop cooking; drain well. Transfer to large bowl.

2. Add salad dressing to pasta and vegetable mixture; toss lightly to coat.
Makes 4 to 6 servings

Diner Egg
Salad Sandwiches

6 eggs, divided
2 tablespoons mayonnaise
1½ tablespoons sweet pickle relish
½ cup finely chopped celery
⅛ to ¼ teaspoon salt
Black pepper
8 slices whole-grain bread

1. Place eggs in medium saucepan. Add enough cold water to cover eggs; bring to a boil over high heat. Immediately reduce heat; simmer 10 minutes. Drain and peel eggs under cold water.

2. Cut eggs in half. Reserve 2 yolks for another use. Place remaining 4 egg yolks in medium bowl; add mayonnaise and relish. Mash with fork until well blended and creamy. Chop egg whites; add to yolk mixture with celery, salt and pepper. Stir until well blended. Divide egg salad among bread to make 4 sandwiches.   *Makes 4 servings*

Southwestern
Salad

1 can (about 15 ounces) black beans, rinsed and drained
1½ cups cooked corn
1½ cups chopped seeded tomato
½ cup thinly sliced green onions
¼ cup minced fresh cilantro
½ cup vegetable oil
2 tablespoons red wine vinegar
1 teaspoon salt
½ teaspoon black pepper

Combine beans, corn, tomato, green onions and cilantro in large bowl. Whisk together oil, vinegar, salt and black pepper. Pour dressing over salad; stir gently to combine. Serve at room temperature or slightly chilled.   *Makes 6 servings*

Marinated Bean and Vegetable Salad

¼ **cup orange juice**
3 **tablespoons white wine vinegar**
1 **tablespoon canola or vegetable oil**
2 **cloves garlic, minced**
1 **can (about 15 ounces) Great Northern beans, rinsed and drained**
1 **can (about 15 ounces) kidney beans, rinsed and drained**
¼ **cup coarsely chopped red cabbage**
¼ **cup chopped red onion**
¼ **cup sliced celery**
¼ **cup chopped green bell pepper**
¼ **cup chopped red bell pepper**

1. Combine orange juice, vinegar, oil and garlic in small jar with lid; shake well.

2. Combine beans, cabbage, onion, celery and peppers in large bowl. Pour dressing over bean mixture; toss to coat.

3. Refrigerate, covered, 1 to 2 hours to allow flavors to blend. Toss before serving. *Makes 8 servings*

*Tip

This salad would be perfect served along with barbecued chicken or grilled salmon.

Pounceole Salad

Prep Time: 5 minutes • **Start to Finish:** 20 minutes

1 can (20 ounces) hominy
2 teaspoons water
1 can (15 ounces) JOAN OF ARC® Kidney Beans or pinto beans,
   drained, rinsed
1 can (15 ounces) yellow corn, drained
½ cup diced red bell pepper
½ cup diced red onion
3 tablespoons ORTEGA® Diced Green Chiles
½ teaspoon salt
½ teaspoon black pepper
½ cup ORTEGA® Original Salsa, Medium

Pour hominy into skillet; add water. Cook over low heat; separate hominy with wooden spoon. Drain well. Place into large bowl. Add beans, corn, bell pepper, onion, chiles, salt and black pepper. Toss to combine well. Stir in salsa. Serve at room temperature or refrigerate for up to 24 hours.

Makes 6 to 8 servings

Variation: For additional color and an intriguing flavor, substitute cooked and shelled edamame for the beans.

ABC Slaw

2 green apples, cut into thin strips
1 package (10 ounces) broccoli slaw with carrots
3 stalks celery, cut into thin slices
1 bulb fennel, cut into thin strips
¼ cup creamy salad dressing
1 tablespoon lemon juice
½ teaspoon red pepper flakes

Combine all ingredients in large bowl; mix well. Chill 1 hour before serving.

Makes 4 to 6 servings

Marinated Tomato Salad

2 cups cherry tomatoes, cut into halves
1 large cucumber, cut in half lengthwise and sliced
1 large yellow or red bell pepper, cut into strips
3 slices red onion, quartered
2 tablespoons balsamic vinegar
1 tablespoon olive oil
½ teaspoon dried basil
½ teaspoon onion salt
¼ teaspoon garlic powder
¼ teaspoon dried oregano

1. Combine tomatoes, cucumber, bell pepper and onion in large bowl.

2. Combine vinegar, oil, basil, onion salt, garlic powder and oregano in small bowl. Pour over vegetables; mix well. *Makes 6 to 8 servings*

Red Bean & Corn Salad with Lime-Cumin Dressing

¼ cup fresh lime juice
1 tablespoon canola oil
1 teaspoon ground cumin
1 teaspoon water
¼ teaspoon salt
1½ cups canned kidney beans, rinsed and drained
1 cup frozen corn with bell pepper and onion, thawed
½ cup chopped tomato
¼ cup chopped green onion, divided
4 large romaine lettuce leaves

1. Whisk together lime juice, oil, cumin, water and salt in medium bowl.

2. Add beans, corn, tomato and 2 tablespoons green onion; toss to coat. Serve on lettuce leaves. Top with remaining green onion.

Makes 2 servings

BLT Salad with Bow Ties & Cheddar

Prep Time: 20 minutes • **Cook Time:** 10 to 16 minutes

2 cups (4 ounces) bow-tie or corkscrew-shaped pasta
1 package (9 ounces) DOLE® Organic Salad Blend Romaine & Radicchio or Baby Spinach Salad
1 cup cherry, pear or baby Roma tomatoes, halved
¾ cup (3 ounces) Cheddar cheese, diced
5 strips bacon, cooked, drained and crumbled *or* ⅓ cup packaged bacon bits
⅓ cup ranch salad dressing

• Cook pasta according to package directions. Drain well and rinse in cool water. Drain again.

• Toss together salad blend, pasta, tomatoes, cheese, and bacon in large bowl. Pour dressing over salad; toss to evenly coat.

Makes 3 to 4 servings

Lime-Ginger Cole Slaw

2 cups shredded green cabbage
1½ cups matchstick-size carrots
1 cup shredded red cabbage
¼ cup finely chopped green onions
3 tablespoons lime juice
2 tablespoons sugar
2 tablespoons chopped fresh cilantro
2 teaspoons vegetable or canola oil
1½ teaspoons grated fresh ginger
⅛ teaspoon salt
⅛ teaspoon red pepper flakes (optional)

Combine all ingredients in large bowl. Toss well. Let stand 10 minutes before serving.

Makes 4 servings

Potato and Blue Cheese Salad

1 pound new or fingerling potatoes
½ teaspoon salt
½ cup shredded radicchio
¼ cup pitted, halved kalamata or niçoise olives
¼ cup (1 ounce) crumbled Gorgonzola cheese
2½ tablespoons olive oil
1 teaspoon Dijon mustard
1 teaspoon white wine vinegar
¼ teaspoon black pepper

1. Place potatoes in medium saucepan; sprinkle with salt. Add water to cover. Bring to a boil and cook about 20 to 25 minutes or until potatoes are tender. Drain well. Cut potatoes into bite-size pieces.

2. Combine potatoes, radicchio, olives and cheese in large bowl. Stir together oil, mustard, vinegar and pepper in small bowl. Pour over potato mixture; toss to coat.

3. Let stand 30 minutes for flavors to blend. Serve at room temperature.

Makes 4 to 6 servings

Variation: Replace Gorgonzola cheese with feta cheese and use sun-dried tomatoes and fresh basil instead of radicchio.

Bock BBQ
Bean Salad

⅓ **cup prepared spicy barbecue sauce**
¼ **cup bock beer**
3 **tablespoons cider vinegar**
1 **tablespoon molasses**
1 **teaspoon hot pepper sauce**
½ **teaspoon mustard seeds**
1 **can (about 15 ounces) pinto beans, rinsed and drained**
3 **plum tomatoes, seeded and coarsely chopped**
4 **stalks celery, halved lengthwise and sliced**
½ **cup chopped green onions**
   Salt
   Black pepper
   Additional hot pepper sauce (optional)
   Large lettuce leaves (optional)

1. Combine barbecue sauce, beer, vinegar, molasses, hot pepper sauce and mustard seeds in large bowl.

2. Add beans, tomatoes, celery and green onions; toss to coat. Season with salt, pepper and additional hot pepper sauce, if desired. Serve in lettuce-lined bowl, if desired.   *Makes 4 to 6 servings*

*Tip

This salad will keep, covered, in refrigerator for up to 2 days. Bring it to room temperature before serving.

German Potato Salad with Grilled Sausage

Prep Time: 15 minutes • Cook Time: 15 minutes

⅔ cup prepared vinaigrette salad dressing
¼ cup *French's*® Spicy Brown Mustard or *French's*® Honey Dijon
   Mustard
1 tablespoon sugar
1½ pounds red or other boiling potatoes, cut into ¾-inch cubes
1 teaspoon salt
1 cup chopped green bell pepper
1 cup chopped celery
½ cup chopped onion
½ pound kielbasa or smoked sausage, split lengthwise

1. Combine salad dressing, mustard and sugar in large bowl; set aside.

2. Place potatoes in large saucepan. Add salt and enough water to cover potatoes. Heat to boiling. Cook 10 to 15 minutes until potatoes are tender. Drain and transfer to bowl with dressing. Add bell pepper, celery and onion. Set aside.

3. Grill sausage over medium-high heat until lightly browned and heated through. Cut into small cubes. Add to bowl with potatoes. Toss well to coat evenly. Serve warm.   *Makes 6 to 8 servings*

*Tip

For zesty baked beans, add ½ cup *French's*® Mustard to 2 (16-ounce) cans pork and beans. Heat and serve.

Salsa Salad Bowl

1 can (about 15 ounces) black beans, rinsed and drained
1 pint grape tomatoes, quartered
4 ounces mozzarella cheese, cut into ¼-inch cubes
½ medium poblano chile or green bell pepper, chopped
½ cup chopped red onion
⅓ cup chopped fresh cilantro
¼ cup lime juice (about 2 medium limes)
1 tablespoon extra-virgin olive oil
¼ teaspoon salt
⅛ teaspoon ground red pepper

1. Combine beans, tomatoes, cheese, chile pepper, onion and cilantro in medium bowl.

2. Combine lime juice, olive oil, salt and red pepper in small bowl.

3. To serve, pour dressing over bean mixture.   *Makes 4 servings*

*Tip

To prepare this salad for transport, place equal amounts of salad in 4 quart-size resealable food storage bags or lidded containers. Stir dressing and put about 1½ tablespoons of dressing in each of 4 small resealable food storage bags. Place the smaller bags inside the larger bags with salad.

Mediterranean Veggie Salad

Prep Time: 11 minutes

2 ounces uncooked whole wheat rotini
½ cup (3 ounces) seeded and diced tomatoes
½ cup (2 ounces) thinly sliced zucchini
½ cup thinly sliced green bell pepper
¼ cup finely chopped red onion
2 tablespoons coarsely chopped pimiento-stuffed green olives
2 to 3 teaspoons cider vinegar
1 teaspoon dried oregano
½ teaspoon dried basil
½ clove garlic, minced
1 teaspoon extra-virgin olive oil
¼ teaspoon salt
½ cup (2 ounces) crumbled feta cheese

1. Cook pasta according to package directions; drain. Rinse under cold water. Drain well.

2. Meanwhile, combine tomatoes, zucchini, bell pepper, onion, olives, vinegar, oregano, basil and garlic in large bowl.

3. Add cooled pasta, oil and salt to tomato mixture; toss gently. Sprinkle with cheese. *Makes 5 servings*

Barley "Caviar"
(p. 104)

Santa Fe Salad
(p. 110)

Quinoa & Mango
Salad (p. 106)

Couscous Turkey Salad
(p. 112)

Great Grains

Barley "Caviar"

4 cups water
½ teaspoon salt, divided
¾ cup pearled barley
½ cup sliced pimiento-stuffed olives
½ cup finely chopped red bell pepper
1 large celery stalk, chopped
1 large shallot, finely chopped
1 jalapeño pepper,* minced, *or* ¼ teaspoon red pepper flakes
2 tablespoons plus 1 teaspoon olive oil
4 teaspoons white wine vinegar
¼ teaspoon ground cumin
⅛ teaspoon black pepper
8 leaves endive or Bibb lettuce

*Jalapeño peppers can sting and irritate the skin, so wear rubber gloves when handling peppers and do not touch eyes.

1. Bring water and ¼ teaspoon salt to a boil in medium saucepan over high heat. Stir in barley. Cover; reduce heat to low. Simmer 45 minutes or until barley is tender. Remove from heat; let stand 5 minutes. Drain, rinse under cold water; drain well. Transfer barley to large bowl.

2. Add olives, bell pepper, celery, shallot and jalapeño to barley.

3. Combine oil, vinegar, remaining ¼ teaspoon salt, cumin and black pepper in small bowl. Pour over barley mixture; stir gently to mix well. Let stand 10 minutes. To serve, divide among endive leaves.

Makes 8 appetizer servings

Quinoa & Mango Salad

2 cups water
1 cup uncooked quinoa*
2 cups cubed peeled mango (about 2 large mangoes)
½ cup sliced green onions
½ cup dried cranberries
2 tablespoons chopped fresh parsley
¼ cup olive oil
1 tablespoon plus 1½ teaspoons white wine vinegar
1 teaspoon Dijon mustard
½ teaspoon salt
⅛ teaspoon black pepper

Quinoa is pronounced keen-wah. This grain is available in health food stores or in the health food aisle of large supermarkets.

1. Combine water and quinoa in medium saucepan. Bring to a boil. Reduce heat; simmer, covered, 10 to 12 minutes or until all water is absorbed; stir. Cover and let stand 15 minutes. Transfer to large bowl; set aside.

2. Add mango, green onions, cranberries and parsley to quinoa; mix well.

3. Combine oil, vinegar, mustard, salt and pepper in small bowl; whisk until blended. Pour over quinoa mixture; mix until well blended.

Makes 8 servings

Note: While quinoa is an ancient grain that was grown by Incas, it is new to most Americans. This tiny round whole grain is higher in protein than other grains. It contains all eight essential amino acids, therefore, it is considered a complete protein.

*Tip

This salad can be made several hours ahead and refrigerated. Allow it to stand at room temperature for at least 30 minutes before serving.

Low-Carb Tabbouleh

¼ cup fine-grain bulgur wheat
¼ cup water
1 tablespoon lemon juice
¼ cup extra-virgin olive oil
1½ cups peeled, seeded and diced cucumbers
1½ cups diced tomatoes (3 medium tomatoes)
1 cup chopped flat-leaf (Italian) parsley
¼ cup sliced green onions
¼ cup chopped fresh mint leaves
2 teaspoons finely chopped walnuts
1 teaspoon finely chopped garlic
Salt to taste

1. Combine bulgur and water in medium bowl; set aside 30 minutes or until all liquid is absorbed.

2. Add lemon juice and olive oil to bulgur; mix well. Stir in cucumbers, tomatoes, parsley, green onions, mint, walnuts, garlic and salt.

3. Chill for at least 2 hours before serving, stirring occasionally.

Makes 6 servings

*Tip

Try serving this tabbouleh with pita bread wedges.

Santa Fe Salad

2 cups cooked brown rice, cooled
1 can (16 ounces) black beans or pinto beans, rinsed and drained
1 can (17 ounces) whole kernel corn, drained
¼ cup minced onion
¼ cup white vinegar
2 tablespoons vegetable oil
2 tablespoons snipped cilantro
2 jalapeño peppers, minced
2 teaspoons chili powder
1 teaspoon salt

Combine rice, beans, corn, and onion in medium bowl. Combine vinegar, oil, cilantro, peppers, chili powder, and salt in small jar with lid. Pour over rice mixture; toss lightly. Cover and chill 2 to 3 hours so flavors will blend. Stir before serving. *Makes 4 servings*

Favorite recipe from **USA Rice**

Couscous Turkey
Salad

Salad
1 cup plus 2 tablespoons chicken broth
¾ cup uncooked pearl or Israeli couscous
1½ cups chopped cooked turkey
1 cup shredded carrots (2 medium carrots)
1 stalk celery, trimmed and finely chopped
1 green onion, trimmed and chopped
2 tablespoons toasted pine nuts*
Salad greens (optional)

Dressing
2 tablespoons jellied cranberry sauce
2 tablespoons vegetable oil
4 teaspoons balsamic vinegar
½ teaspoon curry powder
¼ teaspoon salt
¼ teaspoon pepper

Toast pine nuts in dry skillet over medium-high heat about 2 minutes or until fragrant, stirring constantly.

1. Bring chicken broth to a boil in small saucepan. Stir in couscous; cover and reduce heat to low. Simmer 3 to 5 minutes or until liquid is absorbed and couscous is tender. Remove from heat; set aside.

2. Meanwhile, combine turkey, carrots, celery, green onion and pine nuts in large bowl. Stir in couscous.

3. For dressing, stir together cranberry sauce, oil, vinegar, curry powder, salt and pepper in small bowl. Pour over salad; toss well. Serve on bed of greens, if desired.   *Makes 4 servings*

Note: Israeli couscous, also called pearl couscous, is the size of small pearls and cooks like pasta. If you can't find Israeli or pearl couscous in your supermarket, use plain packaged couscous. Prepare couscous as directed on package, using the amount of chicken broth and salt called for in the recipe.

Spicy Peanut Noodle Salad

Prep Time: 10 minutes

⅓ cup *French's®* **Honey Dijon Mustard**
⅓ cup **reduced-sodium chicken broth**
⅓ cup **peanut butter**
2 tablespoons **reduced-sodium teriyaki sauce**
2 tablespoons *Frank's® RedHot®* **Cayenne Pepper Sauce, or more to taste**
2 cups **thinly sliced vegetables, such as green onion, snow peas, cucumber or bell peppers**
4 ounces **thin spaghetti, cooked and drained (1½ cups cooked)**

1. Combine mustard, chicken broth, peanut butter, teriyaki sauce and *Frank's® RedHot®* Sauce in large bowl; whisk until blended.

2. Add remaining ingredients; toss to coat. Serve immediately. If desired, serve on salad greens. *Makes 4 servings*

*Tip

To serve as a main dish, add 2 cups diced cooked turkey.

Steak, Sugar Snap Pea & Barley Salad

Prep and Cook Time: 50 minutes to 1 hour
Marinate Time: 6 hours to overnight

1 pound beef top round steak, cut 1-inch thick
¼ cup prepared lowfat vinaigrette
2 cups fresh sugar snap peas
2 cups cooked barley
1 cup yellow and red grape or teardrop tomatoes, halved
3 cloves garlic, minced
1 teaspoon pepper

Gremolata Dressing
¼ cup prepared lowfat vinaigrette
2 tablespoons chopped fresh parsley
2 teaspoons grated lemon peel
¼ teaspoon pepper

1. Combine Gremolata Dressing ingredients in small bowl until well blended, refrigerate until ready to use.

2. Place beef steak and ¼ cup vinaigrette in food-safe plastic bag; turn steak to coat. Close bag securely and marinate in refrigerator 6 hours or as long as overnight, turning occasionally.

3. Bring water to boil in large saucepan. Add peas; cook 2 to 3 minutes until crisp-tender. Drain; rinse under cold water. Combine peas, cooked barley and tomatoes in large bowl; toss with dressing and set aside.

4. Remove steak from marinade; discard marinade. Combine minced garlic and 1 teaspoon pepper; press evenly onto steak. Place steak on grid over medium, ash-covered coals. Grill, uncovered, about 16 to 18 minutes for medium rare doneness, turning once. (Do not overcook.)

5. Carve steak into thin slices, season with salt, as desired. Add steak slices to barley mixture.   *Makes 4 servings*

Cook's Tip: To broil, place steak on rack in broiler pan so surface of beef is 2 to 3 inches from heat. Broil 17 to 18 minutes for medium rare doneness, turning once. (Do not overcook.)

Favorite recipe from **The Beef Checkoff**

Fresh Spinach and Couscous Salad with Feta Cheese

1 cup water
¾ cup uncooked whole wheat couscous
1 cup canned white beans, rinsed and drained
1 cup (2 ounces) coarsely chopped spinach leaves, packed
1 can (about 2 ounces) sliced ripe olives, drained
3 slices (1 ounce) hard salami, cut into thin strips
3 tablespoons Greek Vinaigrette (page 151)
3 tablespoons cider vinegar
1 tablespoon dried oregano
1½ teaspoons dried basil
⅛ teaspoon red pepper flakes
3 ounces sun-dried tomato and basil feta cheese, crumbled

1. Pour water into medium microwaveable bowl. Microwave on HIGH 2 to 3 minutes or until boiling. Remove from microwave; stir in couscous. Cover with plastic wrap; let stand 5 minutes.

2. Place couscous in fine mesh strainer. Rinse under cold water until cooled; drain excess water.

3. Combine beans, spinach, olives, salami, vinaigrette, vinegar, oregano, basil and red pepper flakes in large bowl.

4. Add couscous to spinach mixture; stir until blended. Add cheese; toss gently. *Makes 4 servings*

Cook's Tip: To cool couscous quickly, fluff with a fork, spread in a thin layer on a baking sheet, and let stand 5 minutes.

Asian Brown Rice and Peanut Salad Toss

1½ cups water
¾ cup uncooked brown rice
⅔ cup dry-roasted peanuts
1 can (8 ounces) sliced water chestnuts, drained
1 cup snow peas
½ cup chopped red onion
½ cup chopped green bell pepper
¼ cup dried cranberries or raisins
2 tablespoons cider vinegar
2 tablespoons honey
2 tablespoons soy sauce
¼ teaspoon red pepper flakes

1. Bring water to a boil over high heat in medium saucepan. Stir in rice; return to a boil. Reduce heat; simmer, covered, 30 to 40 minutes or until rice is tender and liquid is absorbed. Rinse rice with cold water; drain well.

2. Meanwhile, place small skillet over medium-high heat. Add peanuts; cook and stir 3 to 4 minutes or until fragrant. Transfer to large bowl. Stir in water chestnuts, snow peas, onion, bell pepper and cranberries. Stir in rice.

3. Combine vinegar, honey, soy sauce and pepper flakes in small bowl.

4. Add vinegar mixture to rice mixture; toss to coat.   *Makes 6 servings*

Wheat Berry Apple Salad

1 cup uncooked wheat berries (whole wheat kernels)
½ teaspoon salt
2 apples (1 red and 1 green)
½ cup dried cranberries
⅓ cup chopped walnuts
1 stalk celery, chopped
Grated peel and juice of 1 medium orange
2 tablespoons rice wine vinegar
1½ tablespoons chopped fresh mint
Lettuce leaves (optional)

1. Place wheat berries and salt in large saucepan; cover with 1-inch water. Bring to a boil. Stir and reduce heat to low. Cover and cook, stirring occasionally, 45 minutes to 1 hour or until wheat berries are tender but chewy.* (Add additional water if wheat berries become dry during cooking.) Drain and let cool. (Refrigerate for up to 4 days if not using immediately.)

2. Cut unpeeled apples into bite-size pieces. Combine wheat berries, apples, cranberries, walnuts, celery, orange peel, orange juice, vinegar and mint in large bowl. Cover; refrigerate at least 1 hour to allow flavors to blend. Serve on lettuce leaves. *Makes about 6 cups*

To cut cooking time by 20 to 30 minutes, wheat berries may be soaked in water overnight. Drain and cover with 1-inch fresh water before cooking.

Italian Artichoke and Rotini Salad

4 ounces uncooked whole wheat or tri-colored rotini
1 can (14 ounces) quartered artichoke hearts, drained
½ cup (4 ounces) sliced pimientos
1 can (about 2 ounces) sliced black olives, drained
2 tablespoons finely chopped onion
2 teaspoons dried basil
½ clove garlic, minced
⅛ teaspoon black pepper
3 tablespoons cider vinegar
1 tablespoon extra-virgin olive oil
¼ teaspoon salt

1. Cook rotini according to package directions. Drain pasta; rinse under cold running water to cool completely. Drain well.

2. Meanwhile, combine artichokes, pimientos, olives, onion, basil, garlic and pepper in large bowl.

3. Add pasta to artichoke mixture; toss to blend.

4. Just before serving, combine vinegar, oil and salt; whisk until well blended. Toss with pasta mixture to coat.   *Makes 4 servings*

Quinoa and Shrimp Salad

1 cup uncooked quinoa
6 cups water
½ teaspoon salt, divided
1 bag (12 ounces) cooked baby shrimp, thawed, well-drained
1 cup cherry or grape tomatoes, halved
¼ cup chopped fresh basil
2 tablespoons capers
2 tablespoons finely chopped green onion
3 tablespoons olive oil
1 teaspoon grated lemon peel
1 to 2 tablespoons lemon juice
⅛ teaspoon black pepper

1. Place quinoa in fine-mesh sieve. Rinse well under cold running water. Bring water and ¼ teaspoon salt to a boil in medium saucepan over high heat. Stir in quinoa. Cover; reduce heat to low. Simmer 12 to 14 minutes or until quinoa is tender and plump. Remove from heat. Drain well; set aside to cool to room temperature.

2. Combine quinoa, shrimp, tomatoes, basil, capers and green onion in large bowl. Combine oil, lemon peel, lemon juice, pepper and remaining ¼ teaspoon salt in small bowl. Pour over salad; toss gently to coat.

Makes 4 to 6 servings

*Tip

Soggy shrimp ruin the texture of this salad. To drain shrimp well, place shrimp in a sieve until well-drained or squeeze out excess moisture by hand with paper towels.

**Fresh Spinach-Strawberry
Salad (p. 138)**

**Tart & Tangy Cherry
Salad (p. 139)**

Double Mango Shrimp Salad (p. 132)

Tapioca Fruit Salad (p. 136)

Fresh and **Fruity**

Lemon-Raspberry
Salad

Prep Time: 15 minutes • **Chill Time:** 5 hours 15 minutes

1 package (4-serving size) lemon gelatin
1 cup boiling water
1 cup cold water
1 cup fresh raspberries
   Raspberry Sauce (recipe follows)

1. Place gelatin in large bowl; add boiling water, stirring until gelatin dissolves. Stir in cold water. Cover; refrigerate about 1 hour 15 minutes or until mixture is until slightly thickened.

2. Lightly coat 4 (6-ounce) custard cups with nonstick cooking spray. Stir raspberries into gelatin; spoon evenly into prepared cups. Cover; refrigerate 4 hours or until set.

3. Meanwhile, prepare Raspberry Sauce. Unmold each dessert onto serving plates; drizzle with 2 tablespoons raspberry sauce.

Makes 4 servings

Raspberry
Sauce

1 package (12 ounces) frozen unsweetened raspberries, thawed
1 tablespoon sugar
1 teaspoon fresh lemon juice

1. Place raspberries in fine wire mesh sieve over medium bowl; press berries through sieve, discarding solids.

2. Stir in sugar and lemon juice.

Makes about ½ cup

Fruit
Slaw

1 package (16 ounces) coleslaw mix
1 Granny Smith apple, cut into matchstick strips
1 pear, cut into matchstick strips
1 cup sliced strawberries
⅓ cup lemon juice
2 tablespoons mayonnaise
1 tablespoon sugar
2 teaspoons poppy seeds
1 teaspoon Dijon mustard
¼ teaspoon salt

1. Combine coleslaw mix, apple, pear and strawberries in large bowl.

2. Whisk lemon juice, mayonnaise, sugar, poppy seeds, mustard and salt in small bowl. Pour dressing over cabbage mixture and toss gently. Serve immediately.   *Makes 7 cups*

Simple Citrus
Fruit Salad

¼ cup packed light brown sugar
½ cup freshly squeezed grapefruit juice
1 Texas Rio Star grapefruit, sectioned
2 Texas oranges, sectioned
1 apple, cut into chunks
1 pear, peeled and cut into chunks
1 small pineapple, cut into chunks
1 banana, sliced

Combine brown sugar and grapefruit juice in a large bowl. Add all fruit and toss gently to combine thoroughly. Let sit, covered, at room temperature for about 30 minutes.   *Makes 8 servings*

Favorite recipe from **TexaSweet Citrus Marketing, Inc.**

Double Mango Shrimp Salad

3 tablespoons picante sauce or salsa
1 tablespoon mango or peach chutney
1 tablespoon Dijon mustard
1 tablespoon lime juice
4 cups torn Boston or red leaf lettuce
6 ounces medium cooked shrimp, peeled and deveined
½ cup diced ripe avocado
½ cup diced ripe mango
⅓ cup red or yellow bell pepper strips
2 tablespoons chopped fresh cilantro (optional)

1. Combine picante sauce, chutney, mustard and lime juice in small bowl; mix well.

2. Combine lettuce, shrimp, avocado, mango, bell pepper and cilantro, if desired, in medium bowl. Add chutney mixture; toss well. Serve immediately.   *Makes 2 servings*

*Tip

Try papaya instead of mango in this salad for a change of pace. Just before serving, sprinkle the papaya seeds over the top. They're edible and add a nice peppery punch!

Sweet Potato & Fruit Salad

2 sweet potatoes (8 ounces)
1 small Granny Smith apple, unpeeled and chopped
¼ cup chopped celery
1 container (6 ounces) plain yogurt
2 tablespoons orange juice
½ to 1 teaspoon grated fresh ginger
½ teaspoon curry powder
⅛ teaspoon salt
½ cup cinnamon-coated nuts, divided
¼ cup drained mandarin oranges

1. Pierce sweet potatoes in several places with fork and place on microwavable dish. Cover loosely with microwavable plastic wrap. Microwave on HIGH 6 to 7 minutes, turning once halfway through cooking time. Cool completely.

2. Peel potatoes and cut into 1-inch pieces. Combine potatoes, apple and celery in large bowl.

3. Combine yogurt, orange juice, ginger, curry powder and salt in small bowl. Stir into potato mixture; mix well. Add half of nuts; stir gently. Top with remaining nuts and oranges. Refrigerate until ready to serve.

Makes 4 to 6 servings

Variation: Any type of roasted nut will work great, including honey- or praline-coated.

Tapioca Fruit Salad

1½ cups coconut milk
1 cup milk
¾ cup sugar, divided
2 eggs, beaten
¼ cup water
3 tablespoons quick-cooking tapioca
½ teaspoon vanilla
Pinch salt
1 cup fresh blackberries
1 cup fresh blueberries
2 cups fresh pineapple chunks
2 cups quartered fresh strawberries
1 cup diced mango
Grated peel of 1 lime
2 tablespoons lime juice

1. Mix coconut milk, milk, ½ cup sugar, eggs, water, tapioca, vanilla and salt in medium saucepan. Let stand 5 minutes. Bring to a boil over medium heat, stirring constantly. Remove from heat. Cool 30 minutes. (Pudding will thicken as it cools.) Spoon into individual dessert bowls.

2. Combine fruit in large bowl. Stir in lime peel, juice and remaining ¼ cup sugar; mix well. Spoon over tapioca. Cover. Refrigerate 2 to 3 hours before serving.

Makes 8 servings

Fresh Spinach-
Strawberry Salad

2 to 4 ounces slivered almonds
1 bag (9 ounces) spinach leaves
¾ cup thinly sliced red onion
⅓ cup pomegranate juice
3 tablespoons sugar
3 tablespoons cider vinegar
2 tablespoons vegetable oil
2 tablespoons dark sesame oil
¼ teaspoon red pepper flakes
⅛ teaspoon salt
2 cups quartered strawberries
1 cup (4 ounces) goat cheese, crumbled (optional)

1. Heat medium skillet over medium heat. Add almonds; cook and stir 2 minutes or until lightly browned. Remove from heat; set aside to cool.

2. Meanwhile, combine spinach and onion in large bowl.

3. Combine juice, sugar, vinegar, vegetable oil, sesame oil, pepper flakes and salt in small jar. Secure lid; shake until well blended. Pour dressing over spinach and onion; toss gently to coat. Add strawberries; toss gently. Top with almonds and goat cheese, if desired.   *Makes 5 servings*

Variation: For a refreshing addition, add 1 to 2 teaspoons grated fresh ginger to salad dressing.

Tart & Tangy
Cherry Salad

1 cup lemon-lime soda
1 package (4-serving size) cherry gelatin
1 can (about 14 ounces) pitted, tart red cherries in water
1 can (11 ounces) mandarin orange segments
¼ cup sugar
1 container (8 ounces) whipped topping
¼ cup finely chopped walnuts

1. Pour soda into microwavable 2-cup measuring cup. Microwave on HIGH 1 minute. Transfer soda to large bowl.

2. Whisk in gelatin until completely dissolved. Drain juice from cherries and oranges into gelatin mixture. Stir until well blended.

3. Smash cherries with potato masher or fork. Sprinkle sugar over cherries; mix well.

4. Stir cherry mixture, oranges, whipped topping and walnuts into gelatin until well blended. Pour mixture into glass bowl. Refrigerate 2 hours or until firm. *Makes 10 servings*

*Tip

This recipe is perfect to make the day before and refrigerate overnight.

Citrus-Berry Chicken Salad

Prep Time: 10 minutes • **Cook Time:** 10 minutes

4 boneless skinless chicken breast halves
½ cup *French's*® Honey Mustard, divided
⅓ cup canola oil
2 tablespoons raspberry vinegar or balsamic vinegar
8 cups mixed salad greens, washed and torn
1 cup sliced strawberries or raspberries
1 orange, cut into sections

1. Coat chicken with *¼ cup* mustard. Broil or grill 10 to 15 minutes or until chicken is no longer pink in center. Cut diagonally into slices.

2. In small bowl, whisk together remaining *¼ cup* mustard, oil, vinegar and *¼ teaspoon each salt and pepper.*

3. Arrange salad greens and fruit on serving plates. Top with chicken. Drizzle with dressing just before serving.   *Makes 4 servings*

Fruit Salad with Cherry Vinaigrette

Cherry Vinaigrette
   ½ cup fresh cherries, pitted and chopped
   ¼ cup orange juice
   2 tablespoons balsamic vinegar
   1 to 2 tablespoons honey
   1 tablespoon canola oil
      Pinch of salt

Fruit Salad
   3 cups diced cantaloupe
   1 large mango, peeled and diced
   ¼ cup sliced almonds

1. Combine cherries, orange juice, vinegar, honey, oil and salt in small bowl; set aside.

2. Combine cantaloupe and mango in large bowl. Just before serving, add dressing; toss to coat. Sprinkle with almonds. *Makes 8 servings*

*Tip

For a flavor variation, substitute peaches or nectarines for mango. If fresh cherries aren't available, use thawed and well drained frozen cherries.

Spinach-Melon Salad

6 cups packed torn stemmed spinach
4 cups mixed melon balls (cantaloupe, honeydew and/or watermelon)
1 cup ribbons zucchini*
½ cup sliced red bell pepper
¼ cup thinly sliced red onion
¼ cup red wine vinegar
2 tablespoons honey
2 teaspoons olive oil
2 teaspoons lime juice
1 teaspoon poppy seeds
1 teaspoon dried mint

To make ribbons, thinly slice zucchini lengthwise with vegetable peeler.

1. Combine spinach, melon balls, zucchini, bell pepper and onion in large bowl.

2. Combine vinegar, honey, oil, lime juice, poppy seeds and mint in small jar with tight-fitting lid; shake well. Pour over salad; toss gently to coat.

Makes 6 servings

Cran-Raspberry Gelatin Salad

2 cups boiling water
1 package (4-serving size) cranberry gelatin
1 package (4-serving size) raspberry gelatin
1 can (16 ounces) jellied cranberry sauce
1 tablespoon lemon juice
4 cups frozen raspberries, thawed and drained
1 cup chopped walnuts

1. Coat 1 (2-quart) ring mold or 2 (1-quart) ring molds with nonstick cooking spray; place on baking sheet.

2. Combine boiling water and gelatins in large bowl; stir until dissolved. Melt cranberry sauce in medium saucepan over low heat about 5 minutes. Add cranberry sauce and lemon juice to gelatin mixture; whisk until smooth. Fold in raspberries and walnuts. Pour into prepared mold. Cover and refrigerate about 6 hours or until firm.   *Makes 12 servings*

Pineapple-Lime Salad

2 cans (8 ounces each) crushed pineapple in juice
1 package (4-serving size) lime gelatin
½ cup boiling water
½ cup sour cream
½ teaspoon grated lime peel
1 tablespoon lime juice
2 tablespoons sour cream (optional)

1. Drain pineapple, reserving ⅔ cup juice; set aside. Dissolve gelatin in boiling water. Stir in reserved pineapple juice, ½ cup sour cream, lime peel and lime juice. Cover; refrigerate about 50 minutes or until partially set.

2. Fold pineapple into gelatin mixture. Pour into 8×4 loaf pan. Cover; refrigerate about 4 hours or until firm. Cut into squares to serve. Top each serving with dollop of sour cream, if desired.   *Makes 4 servings*

Salad Dressings

Fresh Raspberry Vinaigrette

- ⅓ cup fresh or thawed frozen raspberries
- ¼ cup vegetable oil
- ¼ cup raspberry or red wine vinegar
- 2 tablespoons sugar
- 2 teaspoons Dijon or honey mustard
- ¼ teaspoon salt
- ¼ teaspoon finely chopped fresh oregano *or* ⅛ teaspoon dried oregano
- ⅛ teaspoon black pepper

Combine all ingredients in food processor or blender. Process until smooth. If dressing is too tart, add additional sugar 1 teaspoon at a time until desired sweetness. *Makes about ¾ cup*

Creamy Garlic Dressing

- ½ cup mayonnaise
- ½ cup sour cream
- Juice of 1 lemon
- 3 cloves garlic, pressed or minced
- 1 tablespoon red wine vinegar
- Salt and black pepper

Combine all ingredients in medium bowl; mix well.

Makes 1 cup dressing

Serving Suggestion: Try this tangy dressing as a dip for vegetables or to dress potato or pasta salad.

Asian Honey Mustard Dressing

¾ cup mayonnaise
2 tablespoons prepared mustard
2 tablespoons honey
2 tablespoons rice wine vinegar
1 teaspoon soy sauce
1 teaspoon dark sesame oil

Combine all ingredients in medium bowl; mix well.

Makes 1 cup dressing

Buttermilk Ranch

¾ cup mayonnaise
½ cup buttermilk
2 tablespoons chopped fresh chives
1 tablespoon chopped fresh parsley
1 clove garlic, minced
1 teaspoon salt
½ teaspoon black pepper

Whisk together all ingredients in small bowl. Refrigerate 30 minutes before serving.

Makes 1¼ cups dressing

*Tip

This dressing can be made with whatever fresh herbs you have on hand. Fresh basil or thyme would work great. If you don't have fresh herbs, use one-third to half of the amount of dried.

Sesame Vinaigrette

2 tablespoons soy sauce
1½ tablespoons dark sesame oil
1 tablespoon water
1 tablespoon balsamic or red wine vinegar
2 teaspoons sugar
1 clove garlic, minced

Combine all ingredients in small jar with tight-fitting lid; refrigerate until serving time. Shake well before using.   *Makes about ½ cup dressing*

Ginger-Teriyaki Salad with
Fried Chicken Tenders, p. 48

Creamy Avocado Dressing

2 ripe avocados, peeled and pitted
Juice of 2 limes
2 tablespoons sour cream
2 tablespoons olive oil
1 teaspoon salt
½ teaspoon ground red pepper
½ teaspoon cumin

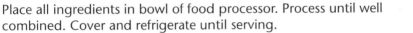

Place all ingredients in bowl of food processor. Process until well combined. Cover and refrigerate until serving.

Makes about 1 cup dressing

Serving Suggestion: Use this dressing to top your favorite Tex-Mex salads or use it as a dip for tortilla chips as a smooth alternative to guacamole.

Greek Vinaigrette

½ cup fresh lemon juice
¼ red wine vinegar
¼ cup chopped fresh oregano
2 cloves garlic, minced
1 teaspoon salt
½ teaspoon black pepper
½ cup olive oil

1. Combine lemon juice, vinegar, oregano, garlic, salt and pepper in medium bowl.

2. Slowly whisk in olive oil until well combined.

Makes 1½ cups dressing

Caesar Dressing

2 tablespoons lemon juice
2 tablespoons sour cream
1 tablespoon red wine vinegar
2 anchovy fillets *or* 1 tablespoon anchovy paste
2 teaspoons Dijon mustard
2 cloves garlic
¾ cup olive oil
¼ cup grated Parmesan cheese

Combine lemon juice, sour cream, vinegar, anchovies, mustard and garlic in food processor. Process until combined. Slowly add olive oil while processing until thickened. Stir in Parmesan cheese.

Makes about 1 cup dressing

*Tip

Anchovies are salty and nutty. They don't have a strong fishy taste and give Caesar dressing its distinctly tangy flavor.

Beef Caesar Salad, p. 43

Lime
Vinaigrette

3 tablespoons finely chopped fresh cilantro or parsley
3 tablespoons plain yogurt
3 tablespoons orange juice
2 tablespoons lime juice
2 tablespoons white wine vinegar
2 tablespoons water
1 tablespoon sugar
1 teaspoon chili powder
½ teaspoon onion powder
½ teaspoon ground cumin

Combine all ingredients in small jar with tight-fitting lid. Shake well.
Refrigerate until ready to use. Shake before serving.

Makes about ¾ cup dressing

Serving Suggestion: Serve with seafood or chicken salads.

The publisher would like to thank the companies listed below for the use of their recipes in this publication.

Courtesy of The Beef Checkoff

Dole Food Company, Inc.

Equal® sweetener

Filippo Berio® Olive Oil

Jennie-O Turkey Store, LLC

Ortega®, A Division of B&G Foods, Inc.

Reckitt Benckiser Inc.

StarKist® Tuna

TexaSweet Citrus Marketing, Inc.

Unilever

USA Rice Federation®

VOLUME MEASUREMENTS (dry)

$^1/_8$ teaspoon = 0.5 mL
$^1/_4$ teaspoon = 1 mL
$^1/_2$ teaspoon = 2 mL
$^3/_4$ teaspoon = 4 mL
1 teaspoon = 5 mL
1 tablespoon = 15 mL
2 tablespoons = 30 mL
$^1/_4$ cup = 60 mL
$^1/_3$ cup = 75 mL
$^1/_2$ cup = 125 mL
$^2/_3$ cup = 150 mL
$^3/_4$ cup = 175 mL
1 cup = 250 mL
2 cups = 1 pint = 500 mL
3 cups = 750 mL
4 cups = 1 quart = 1 L

VOLUME MEASUREMENTS (fluid)

1 fluid ounce (2 tablespoons) = 30 mL
4 fluid ounces ($^1/_2$ cup) = 125 mL
8 fluid ounces (1 cup) = 250 mL
12 fluid ounces (1$^1/_2$ cups) = 375 mL
16 fluid ounces (2 cups) = 500 mL

WEIGHTS (mass)

$^1/_2$ ounce = 15 g
1 ounce = 30 g
3 ounces = 90 g
4 ounces = 120 g
8 ounces = 225 g
10 ounces = 285 g
12 ounces = 360 g
16 ounces = 1 pound = 450 g

DIMENSIONS

$^1/_{16}$ inch = 2 mm
$^1/_8$ inch = 3 mm
$^1/_4$ inch = 6 mm
$^1/_2$ inch = 1.5 cm
$^3/_4$ inch = 2 cm
1 inch = 2.5 cm

OVEN TEMPERATURES

250°F = 120°C
275°F = 140°C
300°F = 150°C
325°F = 160°C
350°F = 180°C
375°F = 190°C
400°F = 200°C
425°F = 220°C
450°F = 230°C

BAKING PAN SIZES

Utensil	Size in Inches/Quarts	Metric Volume	Size in Centimeters
Baking or Cake Pan (square or rectangular)	8×8×2	2 L	20×20×5
	9×9×2	2.5 L	23×23×5
	12×8×2	3 L	30×20×5
	13×9×2	3.5 L	33×23×5
Loaf Pan	8×4×3	1.5 L	20×10×7
	9×5×3	2 L	23×13×7
Round Layer Cake Pan	8×1½	1.2 L	20×4
	9×1½	1.5 L	23×4
Pie Plate	8×1¼	750 mL	20×3
	9×1¼	1 L	23×3
Baking Dish or Casserole	1 quart	1 L	—
	1½ quart	1.5 L	—
	2 quart	2 L	—